CONTENTS

"THE TRUE MYSTERY OF THE WORLD IS THE VISIBLE, NOT THE INVISIBLE."

—OSCAR WILDE

On an otherwise normal summer day in 1977, ten-year-old Marlon Lowe was playing near Kickapoo Creek in Illinois when two monstrous birds appeared in the sky. Before he could run away, one of the beasts dove, grabbed him in its huge claws, and started to fly away. Luckily for Marlon, his mother saw what was happening and came running out of their house to yell at the birds. After carrying him about thirty feet, the enormous bird let Marlon go and flew away with its companion.

Seven other people saw the near-abduction occur, and their descriptions of the birds were all the same: black as crows, with a ring of white feathers around their necks, long beaks that curled downward at the tips, and wings that measured anywhere from eight to ten feet across.

No one in the area—or anywhere else, for that matter—had ever heard of such creatures. It was the first report of an attack by monster birds in the United States. But in earlier times, Native Americans had told stories of a great creature called the Thunderbird, and their stories and paintings resembled the monster that had attacked young Marlon. Could the myths be true, and more importantly, are there still Thunderbirds alive today, perhaps living close to us?

In this book you'll meet a variety of mythical monsters from Bigfoot to the Loch Ness Monster, Thunderbirds to Phantom Cats, the Owlman to the Chupacabra. These creatures have appeared in myths and stories from every country around the world since the beginning of time, and each year more and more people report sightings of them.

BIGFOOT, THE SNOWMAN, 1. AND THE STRANGE APES

From the Nguoi Rung of Vietnam to the Almas of Mongolia, the Yowie of Australia to the Mapinguary of South America, people all over the world have been telling stories of large, hairy, ape-like monsters for thousands of years. And although it's hard to prove whether these creatures truly exist, there are new reports of sightings each year.

BIGFOOT, SASQUATCH, AND YOWIE

In 1958, a construction worker in California named Jerry Crew went to a local newspaper with a plaster cast he had made of a gigantic footprint. Crew explained that he had discovered the print in the mud in a place called Bluff Creek Valley, in Humboldt County. The reason the print caught his attention was its enormous size. The foot that made the print must have been fourteen to eighteen inches long and seven inches wide. The newspaper decided to call the print's maker "Bigfoot," and the name has been used ever since.

Today when people mention Bigfoot, they usually mean the creature seen in the Pacific Northwest area of the United States. But the creature goes by many names. Another popular one is *Sasquatch*, the term commonly used when the creature is sighted in Canada. The name Sasquatch was coined by John W. Burns, a teacher living in British Columbia, who collected stories about the monster from several Aboriginal tribes. He combined the different names they used—from "*sokqueatl*" to "*soss-q'tal*"—and invented the name Sasquatch.

Australians, meanwhile, have their own version of Bigfoot— a creature called the *Yowie*, who appears to live in New South Wales and along the Gold Coast of Queensland. Until the 1970s, he was known by the name the Aboriginals had given him—*Yahoo*—which in their language meant "devil" or "evil spirit." After that, people decided to give him the friendlier name Yowie.

No matter where the creature lives, people always describe Bigfoot the same way. He's almost ten feet tall and completely covered in short, shaggy red or brown hair. In fact, a Bigfoot's color may be the best way to tell the creature's age. A young Bigfoot has a light-colored face, and the hair grows darker as it gets older. Bigfoot is also said to have a small head (for his size), nearly no neck, small and dark eyes, and a thick ridge at his brow.

Of course, Bigfoot's most distinguishing feature is its enormous foot! Bigfoot prints look like human or ape prints, except that they're far too large to be made by either of those animals. In January 2006, a team of scientists led by a man named S. R. Krishnaswamy discovered Bigfoot prints in India that were twenty-nine inches long. Based on the measurements of the prints, the team estimated the creature to weigh over 770 pounds.

Some reports also tell of Bigfoot making high-pitched whis- tles, eerie animal howls, and strange calls that sound like "eek- eek-eek," "sooka-sooka-sooka," and "uhu-uhu-uhu." Among the many spooky recordings is one made in December 2004 by a pilot named John Callender. While exploring a forested area in Mississippi where people had reported seeing strange creatures, he recorded a long, moaning howl that many believe to have come from a Bigfoot.

Although many people claim to have seen Bigfoot, the monsters usually stay far away from humans. When people do happen to see one, it usually doesn't stick around long enough to get caught on film.

KIDNAPPED BY BIGFOOT

In 1924, Albert Osman was prospecting for gold at Toba Inlet, in British Columbia, Canada. He camped alone one night and woke to find that he was being wrapped up in his sleeping bag by a giant monster—it was a Sasquatch, or Bigfoot, who then carried poor Albert away!

When the Bigfoot unwrapped Albert, the two of them were deep in the forest and surrounded by a family of the creatures. To Albert's relief, they were friendly to him, feeding and taking care of him for six days. They even seemed to speak to one another, although Albert couldn't understand their language.

Albert finally managed to escape after he gave the creatures some of his tobacco. The monster tried it, then coughed and struggled to clear its nose and throat. While it was choking, Albert ran away. For years, he kept what had happened to him a secret—he didn't think anyone would believe him. But when more stories of Sasquatch, or Bigfoot, began to surface, and people came looking for the creature near Albert's home, he finally told his tale.

ALTHOUGH MANY PEOPLE CLAIM TO HAVE SEEN BIGFOOT, THE MONSTERS USUALLY STAY FAR AWAY FROM HUMANS. WHEN PEOPLE DO HAPPEN TO SEE ONE, IT USUALLY DOESN'T STICK AROUND LONG ENOUGH TO BE CAUGHT ON FILM.

It does happen, though. In 1967, Roger Patterson and Robert Gimlin set out on a trek through Bluff County, California, to make a documentary about the creature. Still, they were surprised when one of their horses suddenly panicked and reared. Looking up, Roger saw a Bigfoot, and managed to film about 53 seconds of blurry, shaky footage. The film shows a large, hairy figure on two legs walking away from the camera. The figure looks over its shoulder toward the camera and then disappears into the forest. Roger and Robert tracked it for some time, but they never found the creature again.

Since that time, many people have studied the film, and they have different opinions about what it shows. Some think it's a man in a costume, but Hollywood special effects experts disagree. They say the creature looks too real, and that no one could have made a suit like that with the technology available in 1967.

More recently, in April 2005, a local ferry operator in Manitoba, Canada, named Bobby Clarke was taking a barge across the Nelson River when he noticed something strange walking along the shoreline. Luckily, Bobby had a video recorder handy and was able to shoot two minutes and forty-nine seconds of a dark, human-like figure moving on the riverbank. People who have seen the video say the figure is over ten feet tall and matches the description of a Bigfoot.

THE ABOMINABLE SNOWMAN AND THE YETI

For thousands of years, natives of the Himalayas have told stories about a mysterious creature that wanders the mountains of Tibet. Their name for it is *Yeti*, which means "rocky bear" in their

Left: Bigfoot stops to look at Roger Patterson's camera before hurrying away. (THE GRANGER COLLECTION, NEW YORK)

Right: Roger Patterson compares his foot to a plaster cast of a footprint from his supposed Bigfoot sighting. (THE GRANGER COLLECTION, NEW YORK)

language (although there is some dispute over that interpretation—some believe the word translates more accurately into "that thing"). But it wasn't until British explorers began to travel through the region in the 1800s that the rest of the world learned of this monster.

Then in 1921, after a team of explorers reported seeing strange, moving shapes on the side of one of the mountains in Tibet, a man named Henry Newman, who wrote for the *Calcutta Statesman* newspaper, called the creature the *Abominable Snowman*. Many people think that the Abominable Snowman has white fur, but that's just a myth. The team leader, Lieutenant-Colonel C. K. Howard-Bury, described seeing large human-like creatures with long arms and thick black fur. The team later found giant footprints in the snow. The prints were at least three times larger than human footprints.

Sightings continued to grow over the years: In 1951, mountain climber Eric Shipton took pictures of some enormous footprints he found while trying to scale Mount Everest. In 1953, the famous climber Sir Edmond Hillary also reported seeing large footprints in the snow, high up on Mount Everest.

Another climber, Don Whillans, reported seeing a strange creature one night in 1970. He heard sounds in the darkness near his campsite, which his guide (one of the local Sherpa people) said were the call of a Yeti. The next day, Whillans found large footprints in the snow, and later, he spotted a large creature matching the description of a Yeti. He was able to watch it through his binoculars for twenty minutes while it appeared to be looking for food.

THE ALMAS

In the Tien Shan mountain range of Mongolia, a creature known as the *Almas* has been seen since at least the 1400s. Covered with curly red hair, the Almas is only about five feet tall, with a thick eyebrow ridge and jutting jaw. Its name means "wild men" in the Mongolian language. The Almas have been reported as using tools and having their own language, and some scientists believe the creatures might be related to early ancestors of human beings, known as Neanderthals.

THE MAPINGUARY

In South America there lives a creatures known by many as the *Mapinguary* (it's also called *Mapi*, and *Didi*, and sometimes its name is spelled *Mapinguari*). People in the Amazon rainforest have reported seeing it for thousands of years.

Mapi has a bulky body covered with red hair, and makes whistling noises or high-pitched wailing sounds. Although it walks on all fours, the creature stands six feet tall when on two legs, and has a flat snout on its face. Some people say it looks like a giant sloth, while others describe it having a rough, armored skin like an alligator's hide.

When people see a Mapinguary, it's usually an unpleasant surprise—the creature likes to stay away from humans. Witnesses say that it stands in a threatening position when spotted, rearing up on two legs, showing its long claws, and releasing a terrible smell from its belly.

A scientist named David Oren has spent several years collecting stories about the Mapinguary, and his work suggests that the creature might be a descendant of an animal called the Megatherium, which was a sloth the size of an elephant that appears to have gone extinct over 8,000 years ago. Oren also suggested the Mapinguary could be a Mylodon, another giant sloth (smaller than the Megatherium), which became extinct over 10,000 years ago. Animals resembling Mylodons appear in drawings from China that date back to 1430 and on a map from 1513. So perhaps relatives of the giant sloth have managed to survive, after all.

NGUOI RUNG

One unusually friendly monster is the *Nguoi Rung*, which has been spotted in Vietnam, Cambodia, and Laos since the 1970s. The creature goes by many different names, all of which are respectful. Nguoi Rung means "forest people," which is the same name people in Indonesia use for the orangutan. Another name for the monster is Khi Tran, which means "buffalo monkey," or "big monkey."

Covered in gray, brown, or black hair, Nguoi Rung has been seen both alone and in groups. Witnesses describe visits from the creatures at night, when the Nguoi Rung come out of the forest to join people at their fires. The monsters sit next to humans for a short time, but they never speak. They warm themselves at the fire, and then return to the forest.

THE MINNESOTA ICEMAN

A touring exhibition in the late 1960s featured a creature known as the *Minnesota Iceman*, which remains a mystery to this day. Frozen in a block of ice, the Iceman was over six feet tall and covered with long, dark brown hair.

Strangely, the body disappeared in 1968 and was replaced by a model. No one knew what happened to the original creature, and the man who ran the exhibition, Frank Hansen, would only say that the body was owned by a mysterious millionaire.

Before the body vanished, several scientists examined it. Some believed it to be a Bigfoot, while others said it was a Neanderthal that had been discovered in Vietnam and smuggled back to the United States.

BONDEGEZOU

In Indonesian New Guinea, the Moni tribe of Irian Jaya tell stories about the *Bondegezou*. Its name means "man of the forests." The creature is less than three feet tall and looks like a small human, except that its entire body is covered with patches of black and white fur.

One of the strangest parts about the story of the Bondegezou is that no one looked into it seriously until 1994, even though there had been stories about it for hundreds of years and photos since the 1980s. Then, a scientist named Tim Flannery discovered some Bondegezou skin and bones, and realized that the creature was actually a new species. When the discovery was announced, scientists said that the Bondegezou wasn't a mysterious creature like Bigfoot, nor was it an ape of any kind. It was actually a very strange-looking type of kangaroo!

LOY'S APE

In the 1920s, an explorer named Francois de Loys led a team through South America, where they killed a giant ape. A photo taken by the team showed that the ape was about six feet tall.

Unfortunately, the explorers lost the body in their travels, and only the one photo of it exists. The photo is very controversial, and many believe "Loy's Ape" is actually a unique kind of spider monkey (except that it's much larger than any monkey ever seen).

Another ape known as the *Mono Grande* has been seen in South America since the early 1500s. According to eyewitness descriptions, it looks a lot like Loy's Ape. There have been more recent sightings of this strange ape. In 1987, a scientist at a camp in the jungle heard footsteps approaching from behind. When he turned, he saw the creature, which stood five feet tall. It screamed at him and ran away.

SEA MONSTERS: NESSIE
2. AND HER COUSINS

Giant sea serpents, water-bound dragons, or ancient dino-
saurs—sea monsters take many forms, and they're some of the
world's most famous mysterious creatures. For thousands of
years, seafaring explorers have told stories of their encounters
with all sorts of strange creatures. Today, people all over the
world continue to report seeing similar creatures in oceans,
lakes, and other deep, dark bodies of water.

WHAT LIVES IN LOCH NESS?

The largest freshwater lake in Scotland is called Loch Ness, and
it is home to the most famous sea monster that ever lived: the
Loch Ness Monster, also known as *Nessie*. The lake is over twenty
miles long and more than one thousand feet deep, so it is certainly large enough to provide Nessie with room to hide. But the
lake is also narrow—only 1.5 miles wide—so when Nessie does
surface, people on the shore can sometimes spot her and capture
her on film.

According to reported sightings, what the people usually see
of the creature is two or three humps in the water, a long neck,
and a small head, sometimes described as being shaped like a
horse's head. From time to time, people have also seen fins on

the creature's sides, and a long spiky tail. Witnesses say Nessie is anywhere from fifteen to thirty feet long.

The earliest reported sighting of a monster in the lake was long ago, in 565 A.D., by a missionary named Saint Columba, who was crossing the lake when Nessie swam to the surface and approached his boat. The story tells how the saint commanded the monster to leave his boat alone, causing the terrified creature to turn and swim away.

Stories about the monster continued to appear over the centuries, but they really took off in 1933 when a man named George Spicer reported seeing an extraordinary creature cross the road in front of his car. George and his wife said the monster stood about four feet high and was over twenty-five feet long. It slithered across the road and headed into the lake a short distance away. After this story appeared in the *Inverness Courier* newspaper, interest in Nessie grew, along with the number of sightings.

In 1993, there were three different sightings in one night. The first was by Edna MacInnes and David Mackay, who were able to follow the monster as it swam through the lake for ten minutes before it dove back underwater. (MacInnes and Mackay said they had to run along the shore to keep up.) They saw it again about forty minutes later, and a short time after that, James MacIntosh and his son saw the same creature. All of the witnesses described it the same way: pale brown and at least forty feet long, with a long neck held high out of the water. Later that same night, Lorraine Davidson reported seeing large, strange waves in the lake, as if a boat had been crossing the water, but there were no boats anywhere to be seen.

FAMOUS PHOTO/FAMOUS HOAX

The most famous picture of Nessie captivated people for decades before one of its creators finally admitted it was actually a hoax! In 1934, Robert Kenneth Wilson took a photo that shows a long-necked creature that looks a little like a dinosaur known as a plesiosaur. Nearly sixty years later, a man named Chris Spurling told the world that he helped create the photo using a clay figure and a toy submarine.

This famous photo of "Nessie" fooled people for nearly sixty years before the truth finally came out. (© VO TRUNG DUNG/CORBIS SYGMA)

IN 1993, USING COMPUTERS TO EXAMINE TIM'S FILM, A TV DOCUMENTARIAN WAS ABLE TO IDENTIFY SHAPES THAT COULD BE THE BACK PART OF THE MONSTER'S BODY, ALONG WITH TWO REAR FLIPPERS AND TWO MORE HUMPS.

The most famous piece of evidence for Nessie's existence is a film made in 1960 by Tim Dinsdale, who was searching for the monster. Dinsdale was watching the lake with his binoculars when he saw something strange moving through the water. He was able to film the creature for four minutes before it vanished. His film shows a large hump moving across the lake, followed by waves that suggest a large body underwater. In 1993, using computers to examine Tim's film, a TV documentarian was able to identify shapes that could be the back part of the monster's body, along with two rear flippers and two more humps.

Since the 1970s, there have also been several serious scientific searches for Nessie, using submarines and sonar to scan the lake. In 1972, one study using underwater cameras managed to film shapes that resembled a large flipper, connected to an even larger body.

In 1975, another study group snapped underwater photos of what appeared to be the monster's neck and upper body, and they may have even caught a picture of Nessie's face. Unfortunately, all of the pictures were too fuzzy to prove once and for all that Nessie exists.

More recent studies, in 1993 and 2001, used sonar to scan the lake. The detectors caught strange movements underwater, as if something large had just swum past the equipment.

Sea monster, giant snake, a new type of fish, a whale, or a modern-day dinosaur—there are many different ideas about Nessie. No one knows exactly what lives in Loch Ness, but one thing is certain: people continue to report seeing *something* strange there every year.

THE MONSTER IN LAKE ERIE

A creature known as *Bessie*, or *South Bay Bessie*, lives in the southern section of Lake Erie, one of North America's Great Lakes. Another name for the monster is Lem, which stands for *Lake Erie Monster*.

Most reports describe Bessie as thirty to forty feet long, gray, and snake-like. One modern idea about the monster is that it may be a giant fish known as a sturgeon, which can grow to be twenty feet long, weigh 300 pounds, and live to be 100 years old.

One of the earliest recorded sightings of the monster occurred in 1793, when a hunter saw a seventeen-foot-long snake-like creature rising out of the water. And in 1873, a group of railroad workers reported seeing a twenty-foot-long sea serpent in the lake. A few days later, some local farm animals vanished, and people found tracks that indicated something had dragged the animals into the lake. This worried the townspeople so much that they formed a posse to hunt for the monster, although they never found it.

Then in 1887, two brothers from the Canadian side of Lake Erie, near Ottawa, were returning from fishing when they saw something that looked like a gigantic fish, but with long arms. It was on land and struggling to get back into the water. Scared of what they saw, but also eager to catch it, the brothers hurried home to get some rope. By the time they came back, the creature had already made it to the water. But the tracks it left on the beach suggested that it was twenty to thirty feet long.

Bessie caused another big stir in 1993, when she apparently attacked a sailboat on the lake, prompting a local businessman

In this painting, a mysterious sea monster appears on a misty lake.
(© SAM FORENCICH/SOLUS-VEER/CORBIS)

named Tom Solberg to offer a $100,000 reward to anyone who could capture the creature safely and unharmed. No one has yet claimed the reward.

CHAMPY

In Lake Champlain, which touches Vermont, New York, and the Canadian province of Quebec, there lives a monster known as *Champ*, or *Champy*, another snake-like creature that measures at least twenty feet long. Over the years, there have been over three hundred sightings of her. One of the earliest was in 1609 by the famous explorer Samuel de Champlain (the lake's name-sake), who saw the creature as he was preparing to fight Iroquois natives on the shore.

After the Great Lakes, Lake Champlain is one of the largest bodies of water in the United States, and like Loch Ness, it's very deep, making it easy for a monster to hide. Early pioneers in the area knew something strange lived in the water. Newspapers began to report sightings of a large creature in 1819, and there were many more throughout the 1800s. In fact, there were so many that in 1873, and again in 1887, the famous circus showman P. T. Barnum offered $50,000 to the first person who could capture the creature—dead or alive. No one ever claimed the cash.

The most famous encounter with Champy occurred in 1977, when a woman named Sandra Mansi snapped a photo of the creature. Sandra was having a picnic with her family when she noticed something moving in the middle of the lake. It had a dark-colored head and long neck. The sight terrified Sandra and her two children, but she managed to take one picture before taking her kids away to safety.

Scientists who studied Sandra's photo said it wasn't a hoax—she had indeed photographed some kind of creature in the lake. One scientist in particular, a man named Roy Mackel, suggested the creature might be a zeuglodon, which is a type of whale that went extinct twenty million years ago.

Just like the people who live near Loch Ness, the people who live near Lake Champlain have come to love their local monster. In 1983, Vermont even passed a law to protect the creature from harm.

OGOPOGO

Lake Okanagan in British Columbia, Canada, conceals another lake monster, *Ogopogo*, which was first described by the local Salish native tribe, and then by the settlers who began to arrive in the 1800s.

The Salish people call the creature the "great beast of the lake" and "snake in the lake," and their early drawings show a giant serpent in the water. They were so afraid of the creature that they carried animals with them when they crossed the water, so they could feed them to the monster if it attacked.

According to the legends of the Salish people the creature later called Ogopogo started off as a man who became possessed by a demon. After he killed a member of the tribe, the gods punished the killer by turning him into a giant snake and confining him to the lake.

Like other lake monsters, Ogopogo is a long, snake-like creature, usually described as being forty feet long and having dark skin. Some reports say Ogopogo has fins on her back and a mane on her head.

There have been many sightings of Ogopogo over the years—in 1989 the creature was caught on film by Ken Chaplain. He was filming his father, who was describing where he had seen the monster, when suddenly it appeared! Their film shows a long, snaky animal swimming in the lake, splashing, and even flicking its tail.

Then in 2000, a marathon swimmer named Daryl Ellis swam the eighty-mile length of the lake to raise money for cancer research. During his swim, he noticed two long, grayish-black creatures swimming beneath him. They came close enough for Daryl to see that their eyes were as large as grapefruits. The creatures didn't attack, but the sighting left Daryl scared. When he swam the lake again the following year, he kept his goggles off so he wouldn't be able to see the beasts.

MONSTER OR SECRET SUB?

In the 1940s, people began to see something strange in Idaho's Lake Pend Oreille. They soon named the creature *Paddler*, or the *Pend Oreille Paddler*. Witnesses said it was long and dark (like other sea serpents), but then a rumor grew that it was actually a secret navy submarine that was being tested in the lake! There were naval stations nearby, but the navy has always denied that they ever tested submarines in Lake Pend Oreille. Nevertheless, the monster hasn't been seen since the war years of the 1940s.

CREATED BY TROLLS?

Across the ocean in Sweden is a creature named *Storsjoodjuret*, which lives in the 300-foot-deep Lake Storsjön, in the north-western province of Jämtland. Known for making a strange sound, like two pieces of wood being clapped together, this monster reportedly has feet, a horse-like head, a long neck, big eyes, and a large mouth. Witnesses usually report seeing three humps in the lake, and they say the creature is from nine to twenty-four feet long.

One of the earliest reports of the monster came in 1635, when a man named Mogens Pedersen wrote down a legend he had heard about the lake. According to the story, two trolls named Kata and Jana had spent many years boiling a magical concoction in a large kettle on the shore of the lake. One day, they heard groans and wails coming from the kettle, and it began to shake. Suddenly it exploded, and a strange animal with the body of a snake and the head of a cat jumped out of the kettle and into the lake.

Over time, the creature grew large enough to wrap itself all the way around the island of Froson, in the middle of the lake. After years of scaring the people who lived nearby, a warrior named Ketil Runske (in some stories his name is Gudfast), managed to imprison the creature using a magical spell carved into a stone, which he placed on Froson. When the stone was broken in the seventeenth century (no one knows how that happened), so many strange sightings took place in the waters of the lake, and the monster disturbed so many people traveling across it, that the residents finally repaired the stone—and it stands to this day.

ACCORDING TO THE STORY, TWO TROLLS NAMED KATA AND JANA HAD SPENT MANY YEARS BOILING A MAGICAL CONCOCTION IN A LARGE KETTLE ON THE SHORE OF THE LAKE. ONE DAY, THEY HEARD GROANS AND WAILS COMING FROM THE KETTLE, AND IT BEGAN TO SHAKE.

But even fixing the stone didn't stop the strange events, for despite its origins as a myth, people continue to report seeing something strange in the lake every year. In 1996 a man named Gun-Brit Widmark even videotaped images on the lake that appear to show humps and a shape thirty to forty feet long.

There have been several searches and even hunting expeditions for the creature over the years, too. Finally in 1986, the local government decided to put Storsjoodjuret on an endangered species list to protect it from harm.

THE GLENADE LAKE MONSTER

An ancient creature lives in Ireland's Glenade Lake: the *Dobhar-Chu*, which means "water hound" in Gaelic. A cross between a dog and an otter, with pure white fur, black ear-tips, and a black cross-shape on its back, the creature is known for growing legs to go hunting on land when it's hungry. According to legend, it could be fatal just to lay eyes on one of these creatures.

The Glenade Stone in Kinlough, Leitrim (also known as the Kinlough Stone), is an old tombstone that shows a picture of the Dobhar-Chu. Writing on the stone tells the story of a woman named Grace who was killed by the monster in 1722 as she was washing clothes in the lake. According to legend, Grace's husband heard her scream, and ran to help, but he arrived too late. He found the Dobhar-Chu lying on her bloody clothes and slew the beast, but before it died it whistled toward the water and another Dobhar-Chu swam toward them. The second creature chased the husband and another man for some time before they finally managed to kill it.

This 1860 illustration from *Harper's Weekly* shows a sea monster supposedly spotted in Hungary Bay, Bermuda. (© CORBIS)

THE BUNYIP

A legendary sea creature named the *Bunyip* lives in Australia, where the Aboriginal people have told stories about it for hundreds, perhaps even thousands, of years. According to the stories, the Bunyip comes in many different shapes and sizes—some are covered in feathers, while others have scales like a crocodile. Most Aboriginal drawings show the Bunyip with a tail like a horse, and flippers and tusks like a walrus.

In the Aboriginal stories, the Bunyip is a spirit that lives in rivers, lakes, swamps, and billabongs—the parts of rivers left behind after the river changes its course. Like many other mythical monsters, the Bunyip doesn't like to be near humans, and it defends the waters where it lives by eating people who come too close. Sometimes it even hunts for people at night, if it's hungry enough. Whenever the Aboriginals heard its cry, they knew to stay away from bodies of water.

Early European settlers in Australia began to report sightings of the Bunyip in the 1800s, mostly in the area of New South Wales. Witnesses described a sea creature with a face like a dog (some said its head was shaped like a horse's), and a body covered with a long shaggy coat of black hair. In 1872, a shepherd saw a strange beast swimming quickly through the waters of Midgeon Lagoon, which he said looked like a giant black dog with no tail and large ears. Sightings continued into the 1930s, when people reported seeing strange creatures in the water near the large hydroelectric dams that were being built at the time.

Since then, the number of sightings has diminished greatly. One theory is that the creatures lived in swamps and bodies of water that have now been drained, so the Bunyips have either died or moved away.

THUNDERBIRDS AND
3. THINGS WITH WINGS

Flying monsters have appeared in the skies over different parts of the earth for thousands of years, so say the myths and legends of many countries. Some of them hunt humans, but there are others that seem to want to help us, warning people of danger and helping them escape from disaster. Either way, when something large, dark, and mysterious descends on you from the sky, it's always a scary matter.

BIRD OR DINOSAUR?

Perhaps the most famous flying monster is the *Thunderbird* of North America, which has been spotted across the United States and Canada. Dark-colored, with a wingspan of at least fifteen feet, Thunderbirds are often said to glide like a giant condor.

The name Thunderbird comes from the ancient belief that the enormous flapping wings of the legendary creature caused the sounds of thunder when it flew. Many stories told by native tribes describe the Thunderbird as having a wingspan as long as two canoes. When it flies, the Thunderbird causes storms by pulling clouds together with its flapping wings, and it also flashes lighting from its eyes. In some Native American stories, the Thunderbird delivers messages for the gods, while in other stories the monster can shape shift, and even take human form.

In almost all the legends, Thunderbirds are dangerous and smart creatures, and people try very hard not to make them angry.

But the Thunderbird doesn't exist in legend alone. According to one newspaper report, two cowboys in Arizona killed a giant flying creature in 1890. The creature had smooth skin and wings like a bat, but its face was like an alligator. Fully stretched out, its wings covered the length of a barn.

Then in 1976, two children playing in their backyard in the Rio Grande Valley of Texas saw a strange figure in the field nearby. Looking at it through binoculars, they discovered that it was actually a huge black bird, at least five feet tall, with red eyes and a beak six inches long. And it was staring back at them. When it made a loud, shrieking sound and started to approach them, the children ran inside until it flew away.

A short time later, a man in Brownsville, Texas, named Alverico Guajardo saw a creature in the sky that looked like a giant bat. He heard its leathery wings flapping, and then two claws tore into the back of his shirt. According to Alverico, the monster had a face like a monkey, with no beak at all. He managed to run and hide under a tree, and eventually the beast flew away.

After this flurry of sightings, the monsters seemed to disappear, and they stopped scaring the people of Texas. But reported sightings of similar flying monsters continue to this day. In 2002, people living in the Alaskan villages of Togiak and Manokotak reported seeing a giant black creature flying overhead with a wingspan of nearly fourteen feet—the size of a small airplane.

Some scientists believe these creatures might be rare giant condors or eagles, but there are others who suggest they could be a type of dinosaur such as a pterodactyl!

THE AHOOL

Resembling a giant bat, the *Ahool* has been seen in the Salek Mountains of Java since 1925, when one of them flew over the head of an explorer named Ernest Bartels. The creature made a sound like "Ahool!" which is the name given to it by the native people of that region.

Witnesses describe the Ahool as being the size of a human child. It has dark grey skin (some say it's covered with gray fur), a head like an ape, huge black eyes, large claws, and leathery wings that are nearly twelve feet long from tip to tip. By comparison, the world's largest "real" bat (according to science), the flying fox of New Zealand, has a wingspan of only six feet.

The Ahool lives in caves behind waterfalls, and flies across the water at night to catch fish with its giant claws. Because of its monkey-like face, some scientists believe the Ahool might be the world's only species of flying ape. To this day, people are still searching for undeniable proof of its existence.

THE OVERWHELMER OF BOATS

Another dinosaur-like flying monster is the *Kongamato*, whose name means "overwhelmer of boats." It's been seen throughout the sub-Saharan area of Africa, especially in the Jiunda swamps of Zambia and Kenya. Also described as being like a giant bat, the Kongamato has large teeth, red leathery skin, and a wingspan of four to seven feet.

One of the earliest descriptions of the Kongamato came in 1923, when a man named Frank Melland wrote a book about Africa and included descriptions of the monster he had learned about from members of the Kaonde tribe of Zambia. Melland showed them a drawing of a pterodactyl dinosaur, and they said it looked exactly like the Kongamato.

In 1932, a team of explorers reported being attacked by one of these creatures, which swooped down on the men while they were at camp. After a few passes, the creature vanished into the night. Then in 1956, an engineer named J. P. F. Brown reported seeing two Kongamato, each with a wingspan of about three feet, visible teeth, a tail, and a face like a dog.

As you can guess from its name, the "overwhelmer of boats" is known for attacking people on the water. The Kaonde tribe even has a magic spell that uses the creature's name: "*muchi wa kongamato*." It's a charm to protect travelers from floods caused by the monster.

MYSTERIOUS WARNINGS

From 1854 to 1856, during the Crimeon War fought in what is the present-day Ukraine, soldiers reported seeing a strange creature in the sky—a gigantic, headless, crow-like animal—soaring in tight circles above them before they were to go into battle. The soldiers were so shocked and afraid that they lost their bearings and ran toward their own army, which mistook them for enemy soldiers and fired at them!

Another winged monster appeared in China in 1926. People reported seeing a "man-dragon," a huge black creature, flying over the Xiaon Te Dam in southeastern China. Days later, the dam collapsed, creating a huge disaster. Many survivors said the man-dragon appeared again on the day of the accident.

The *Freiburg Shrieker* is another strange case of a winged creature appearing just before a disaster. In 1978, workers at a coal mine in Freiburg, Germany, found the entrance to the mine shaft blocked by a mysterious and terrifying black figure with outstretched wings. Several men tried to approach it, but they ran away when the monster let out a series of loud screams. An hour later, there was a huge explosion underground and the mine collapsed. When the men returned to the mine shaft, the Shrieker had disappeared.

A similar creature appeared in the sky of the Ukraine in 1986. Four employees in Chernobyl reported seeing a large, dark, headless man with huge wings and red eyes. A few days later, there was an explosion at the city's nuclear reactor. Workers later recalled seeing a giant bird flying through the smoke.

MANY PEOPLE CLAIMED TO HAVE SEEN THE CREATURE ON WEST VIRGINIA'S SILVER BRIDGE WHEN IT COLLAPSED IN 1967. THEY ALSO REPORTED SEEING IT BEFORE THE ACCIDENT, AND RECEIVING STRANGE WARNINGS ABOUT THE CRASH.

These winged messengers of doom may all be versions of the same creature: the *Mothman*, which appeared in the Point Pleasant area of West Virginia in 1966 and 1967. But Mothman sightings actually date back to the 1800s in New York, Kentucky, Illinois, Nebraska, and Washington State.

Witnesses describe the Mothman as being human-sized, but with wings and gleaming red eyes. One of the strangest aspects of the Mothman story is that it always seems to appear just before terrible accidents or natural disasters such as earthquakes or airplane crashes. People have also seen unidentified flying objects, or UFOs, and other odd lights in the sky at the same time, and in the same area, as Mothman sightings.

Several eerie and ghostly events took place during the time of the Mothman encounters in Point Pleasant. Some of the weirdest reports included doors opening and closing on their own, and locking and unlocking by themselves; loud banging noises on the rooftops at night; and the sounds of a baby crying where no baby seemed to be. In other cases, televisions would flicker and show strange shapes, and people would hear static on their phones that sounded like ghostly human voices. In fact, many people claimed to have seen the creature on West Virginia's Silver Bridge when it collapsed in 1967. They also reported seeing it before the accident, and receiving strange warnings about the crash.

Some people believe the Mothman is a mutant or hybrid animal (such as the rare eagle-owl), but one of the most popular ideas is that it's an "ultraterrestrial," a creature that lives in another universe, in a different dimension, and that has a mysterious (and possibly sinister) purpose for appearing on our planet.

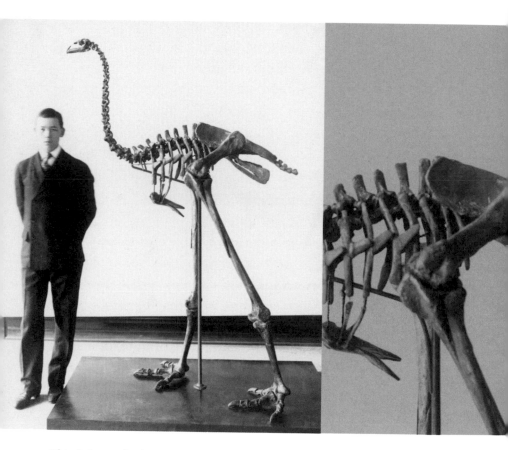

This skeleton of a Great Moa, on display at the National Museum of Natural
History in the early twentieth century, towers over the figure of a full-grown man.
(THE GRANGER COLLECTION, NEW YORK)

EXTINCT OR NOT?

Unlike the other creatures in this chapter, the *Moa* is without a doubt a real animal: a six-foot tall bird with a long neck (the neck is three feet long on its own), and a small head and beak. Its body is covered in reddish-brown and grey feathers, and like the ostrich, emu, and kiwi, the Moa can't fly.

The strange thing about this bird is that it went extinct over 500 years ago, yet people continue to report sightings of it in the forests of New Zealand, where it used to live. Before it went extinct, there were eleven different species of Moa, with the largest reaching nearly ten feet tall and weighing 550 pounds.

The first modern sighting of a Moa happened in 1958, and it's been seen (but never captured) regularly since then. Photos exist from a 1993 sighting, but the images are blurred and it's hard to tell for sure whether or not the creature actually is a Moa. Today, people continue to search for the bird to learn its secret: how did it manage to come back from extinction after 500 years?

PHANTOM CATS AND
4. FELINE MONSTERS

For years, people around the world have reported seeing strange cats, the size of panthers or mountain lions, but they appear in places where no such cats live, and sometimes they look like no known cats on earth. As a group, these creatures are called *Phantom Cats*, or *Alien Big Cats*. Most have been seen in Britain, Australia, New Zealand, and Hawaii, but there are also (less frequently) reports from the United States, Africa, and across Europe.

THE SURREY PUMA

Starting in 1959, a creature called the *Surrey Puma* caused quite a stir in the area of Surrey, England, when a man named A. Burningham saw a dark-colored cat cross the road in front of his car. The cat was huge, like a jungle cat. This might not have been so strange if not for the fact that big cats like that don't live in England. By 1962, many more people had reported seeing this creature. In one sighting, a man named Ernest Jellett described seeing a huge cat with a round, flat face chase a rabbit. The cat had a long, thin tail and big paws. More sightings followed over the next year, including one where the enormous cat jumped over the hood of a police car. People in the area also began to report hearing strange howling at night. Then something started to hunt and kill local farm animals, and large paw prints began to appear in the area.

As these reports persisted throughout the 1960s, authorities continued to deny that there was a wild animal in the Surrey countryside. Instead, they said the incidents might be due to some wild puma cubs that had been released in the area.

Over the years, the number of sightings fell, until the late 1970s and early 1980s, when several new reports of giant cats appeared, along with an entirely new set of feline creatures in the 1990s.

WHO LET THE CATS OUT?

Many people believe the phantom cat population in the United Kingdom grew after a law was passed in 1976 outlawing exotic pets. At the time, it was considered fashionable for the wealthy to keep unusual animals as pets, and big cats were some of the most popular choices. To control this, the government passed the Dangerous Wild Animals Act, which restricted the animals that people could keep as pets. Under the new law, owners of big cats either had to build expensive homes for the animals or find a zoo that would take them—but all the zoos were full. Years later, many of the big cat owners admitted that they had simply released their animals into the wild. Since then, wild cats appear to have been living and breeding in the British countryside.

PEOPLE IN THE AREA ALSO BEGAN TO REPORT HEARING STRANGE HOWLING AT NIGHT. THEN SOMETHING STARTED TO HUNT AND KILL LOCAL FARM ANIMALS, AND LARGE PAW PRINTS BEGAN TO APPEAR IN THE AREA.

THEY DID NOT FIND ANY DEFINITE PROOF OF THE MONSTER, BUT THEY ALSO SAID THEY COULDN'T PROVE IT DIDN'T EXIST.

THE GREAT BEASTS OF ENGLAND

A strange, cat-like creature known as the *Beast of Exmoor* prowls the fields around Devon and Somerset, in England. According to witnesses, the creature is the size of a cougar, or a panther—four to eight feet long—and it has dark or tan-colored fur.

Reports of beast sightings began in the 1970s, and became more popular after an encounter in 1983, when it apparently hunted down over a hundred sheep from the same farm in just three months. By 1988, enough people had seen it, and it had killed enough of the farmers' livestock, that the government sent the Royal Marines to the Exmoor Hills to find the beast.

A few soldiers reported seeing something mysterious in the area, but no one was ever able to catch or even identify it for certain. The government recalled the Marines from this mission (and decided that the creature must have been a hoax because they couldn't find it), but reports of attacks on farm animals increased, and continued over the next several years.

In the late 1990s, a cousin to this creature, the *Beast of Bodmin Moor*, appeared in the southwestern English city of Cornwall, in the area of Bodmin Moor. So many people reported seeing this mysterious cat—and so much livestock had been eaten by an unidentified creature—that in 1995 the British government started an official investigation into it. Unfortunately, they did not find any definite proof of the monster, but they also said they couldn't prove it *didn't* exist.

A few days after the government gave its report, a fourteen-year-old boy named Barney Lanyon-Jones found a large cat skull floating near Bodmin Moor, in the River Fowey. The skull was missing its lower jaw, but two large, sharp teeth could still be seen. Scientists confirmed that it had belonged to a leopard, and said that it had probably been part of a leopard-skin rug that someone had imported. By strange coincidence, two other cat-like skulls were also found in that area in 1988 and 1993.

AMERICA'S PHANTOM CAT

People living in the midwestern and eastern United States have been seeing mysterious cats for over a hundred years—including *Nellie*, a large female lion that was first spotted in Decatur, Illinois, in 1917. The lion's attack on a man named Thomas Gullett, who was working in his boss's garden, sent people looking for her in groups of as many as 300. The huge groups found enormous paw prints, and they saw her several times, but no one managed to catch her. Her ability to escape quickly turned her into a sensation in the region, and the local newspaper nicknamed her "Nellie."

A few days after Nellie attacked Gullett, she went after another four people in their car. She crashed into the side of the vehicle and seemed to knock herself unconscious. The people escaped and brought back the police, but Nellie had woken up and vanished into the night, and she has been seen only rarely since then.

Phantom cats continue to cause a lot of debate. Scientists say it's impossible for such creatures to live in the areas where they have been seen (because of the weather, the types of food available, and the number of humans living close by), and they argue that there's no real proof that they exist.

Others disagree, and in their search for creatures like Nellie, they've named them *Panthera Atrox*, which means "cruel lion" or "fearsome lion" in Latin. This name refers to all of the big mysterious cats people have seen in North America. Larger than African lions, they look like the kind of large cat that went extinct in the last ice age, although some people believe these cats survived in North America, and Nellie could be one of them.

We know about the prehistoric American lion—also known as the North American or American cave lion—from the fossils it left behind. It's about the same size as the Eurasian cave lion, which was the largest cat that ever existed, even bigger than the modern African lion! It was over eleven feet long and weighed over 500 pounds.

It's interesting to note: the American lion also had the largest brain compared to its body size of any lion, living or dead. This might explain why its modern descendants (like Nellie) are so good at hiding from people and remaining a mystery.

BLUE TIGERS

China has its own phantom cats, the most famous of which are the *Blue Tigers*. In 1910, a hunter and missionary named Harry Caldwell saw something strange in the province of Fujian, in the Futsing region. According to Caldwell, he saw a figure that he thought was a man in a blue robe, standing in a field. As he approached, however, Caldwell saw that it was actually a large cat that looked like a tiger, except its fur was dark blue, with darker blue stripes. Before Harry could get any closer, the tiger ran away.

5. OWLMAN, GIANT TURTLES, AND OTHER BIG BEASTS

Many mysterious creatures look like nothing else on earth—but around the world there's also another type of monster. It looks familiar—like an owl, turtle, snake, monkey, or pig—with one huge difference: it is gigantic!

OWLMAN

Throughout the late 1970s, a giant owl appeared in the skies over the village of Mawnan, in Cornwall, England, and people quickly named it the *Owlman* (other names for it are the *Cornish Owlman* and the *Owlman of Mawnan*). Witnesses described it as the size of a human, with pointed ears, large black claws on its feet, and light gray or white feathers. He was said to make a strange hissing sound. Some of the scariest things about him (as if all that wasn't enough) were his glowing red eyes.

The Owlman mystery began in 1976, when two young sisters named June and Vicky Melling went on vacation with their parents and saw the creature flying over the church in Mawnan. The sight scared them so much, their parent cut the holiday short so they could go home.

Three months later, two teenagers, Sally Chapman and Barbara Perry, went camping in Mawnan. As Sally Chapman stood outside her tent, she saw a strange figure flying over the

THERE WERE THREE TIMES AS MANY DOG ATTACKS THAN BEFORE, AND SWIMMERS REPORTED BEING ATTACKED BY DOLPHINS.

local church. More sightings followed over the next few years, all around the church and its graveyard.

Then the local animal life started to act strangely. In one case, hundreds of birds began to attack a woman, who had to run inside her house for protection. Trying to get to the woman, the birds flew into the side of the building hard enough to destroy themselves. In another case, cats chased a woman into her home.

Even more strange animal behavior followed. There were three times as many dog attacks than before, and swimmers reported being attacked by dolphins. Dolphins also saved other swimmers from drowning, and there were sightings of UFOs, sea monsters, phantom cats, and of course, the Owlman.

Owlman sightings peaked between 1976 and 1978, but there have been other sightings since then. In 1989, a young couple encountered the creature as they walked on the road through the Mawnan woods. They saw it sitting on a large tree branch and staring at them with its red eyes. When it leapt off the tree and started to fly toward them, they both ran away in fright.

Then in 1995, an American biology student on vacation in England went for a walk through the woods near Mawnan and saw the Owlman flying above the trees. It terrified her, and she ran away to safety when the creature flew down toward her.

One theory about these strange sightings says the church is built on a "ley line"—a straight line that connects several ancient sites around the world. According to this theory, the Owlman may be a mystical creature that travels from site to site.

Other people think Owlman might be a cross between an eagle and an owl, known (obviously) as an eagle-owl. This rare breed of bird can grow to more than two feet long, with a wing-span of six feet. But of course, this theory doesn't explain the other strange happenings over the years.

THE BEAST OF BUSCO

In Vietnam, there is a legend about a giant golden turtle that lives in Hoan Kiem Lake. According to the story, the turtle gave a magical sword to the emperor in the mid-fifteenth century, which he used to defeat invaders from the north in battle. Afterward, as the emperor was traveling back across the lake to return the sword, the turtle came up out of the water, took the sword from the emperor's hands, and disappeared back below the waves. Since then, the lake has been known as Ho Hoan Kiem, which means "Lake of the Returned Sword."

This story remained simply a legend until 1996, when witnesses saw a gigantic turtle in the lake. Its head was green and yellow, and as large as a football. Then in 1998 there were more sightings, with as many as three turtles being seen at the same time. By then, scientists were very interested and, in fact, they continue to search the lake for the giant golden turtle to this day. Perhaps one day they will also find the magic sword.

Giant turtles have also appeared in other parts of the world. In 1883, sailors on a ship in Grand Bank, in Newfoundland, Canada, saw a turtle that was thirty feet wide and forty feet long, with flippers that were twenty feet long. In 1956, in nearby Nova Scotia, a ship encountered a huge turtle forty-five feet long, with flippers fifteen feet long and a white shell.

But perhaps the most famous giant turtle of all is the *Beast of Busco*, or *Oscar*, as the local people call him.

In 1898, a farmer in Churubusco, Indiana named Oscar Fulk saw a giant turtle living in the lake on his property. No one believed him, and he decided to leave the turtle alone. Many years later, after he sold the farm, the giant turtle was seen again by the new family on the land. They, too, decided to leave it alone. More time passed, and by 1948 the farm had a new owner once more. The farm's new owner saw the turtle twice that year, but then the creature stayed hidden for another year.

The turtle reappeared in 1949, and several people saw it. News of the animal traveled quickly, and many newspapers began to write about it. One paper nicknamed it "Oscar," and another coined the name "The Beast of Busco." People came to the town from all over to catch a glimpse of the creature.

Many people tried to catch Oscar, but all of their attempts failed. When they made a trap, the beast broke free. They tried to drain the lake, but Oscar managed to escape. Some people believed he swam away through an underground tunnel to another body of water. After some time, the lake filled up again and the farm was sold once more.

The native people in that area, who are called the Miami tribe, also have a legend about a giant turtle that helps them to fish by acting as a dock for their boats. Some people believe the turtle in the legend—and Oscar—are types of alligator snapping turtles, which can grow to be quite large (though not as large as the turtles in the stories). Alligator snappers live underwater, and almost never come onto land except to lay eggs. They don't swim, either, but like to walk on the bottom of a body of water.

No one was ever able to catch the Beast of Busco, but the town remembers him (and waits for his return) by celebrating each June with their Turtle Days festival, when they have a parade, a carnival, and turtle races.

THE LUSCA AND THE KRAKEN

In the Pacific Ocean lives a creature called the giant octopus, which can grow to thirty feet long. But there's another creature that many people believe to be a cousin to the Giant Octopus, which makes it look tiny by comparison. In the Bahamas, near the island of Andros, there lives a creature called the Lusca. Although it's rarely seen, witnesses describe it as a gigantic octopus (some even say it's half-octopus, half-shark) anywhere from 75 to 200 feet long! The Lusca live in underwater caves often called "blue holes," and like many smaller octopuses, they can change their color.

Some people believe the Lusca are behind the mysterious creatures known as *Globsters*: huge globs of strange, unidentifiable flesh and bone that have washed up on shores around the world since 1896. They may also be responsible for a strange phenomenon call the Bloop, an ultra-low-frequency sound that was detected by scientists in 1997. It matches the type of sound that an animal would make, but no known creature could make such a sound, unless the animal was very, very large—even bigger than the biggest whale we know about.

The Lusca may also be related to the *Kraken*, another gigantic sea monster that's been seen near Norway and Iceland since at least the 1700s (although there have been reports of strange squid-like creatures in the 1600s and even as early as the 1200s). Early witnesses described the animal as a gigantic squid, the size of a small island. Sailors worried their ships would be sucked down in the whirlpool the Kraken created when it dove underwater.

Throughout the 1800, scientists and sailors tried to capture a Kraken, but the closest anyone came was in 1873, when a Canadian fisherman managed to cut off part of a tentacle from one of the creatures. Scientists determined the entire arm must have been thirty feet long, and the entire creature over sixty feet long.

In 1880, a sixty-five-foot-long giant squid washed up on shore in New Zealand. Although witnesses report seeing squid as large as ninety feet long, the creature remained steeped in mystery until 2004, when scientific teams from Japan caught the first-ever images of a giant squid (nearly thirty feet long) in the ocean. Now the world knows giant squid exist for real, and the legends of the Lusca and Kraken have come to life.

A scuba diver goes for a swim with a giant octopus.
(© JEFFREY L. ROTMAN / CORBIS)

In this nineteenth-century wood engraving, the Kraken attacks a ship at sea.
(© BETTMANN/CORBIS)

GIANT SHARKS

In the waters off New Zealand resides one of the most fearsome sea creatures that ever lived: the giant shark. Most people believe that the *Megalodon*—the prehistoric ancestor of the modern shark—went extinct 1.5 million years ago. But there is evidence to suggest that it still survives, such as two huge shark teeth (about five inches long) found in Megalodon fossils by the HMS *Challenger*, the ship that carried out the first marine research expedition in 1858. The problem is, the newer teeth are only 11,000 years old, which means that some Megalodons must have survived the extinction. Some may still live in the oceans today. In 1918, fishermen in New Zealand saw a white shark that was over 100 feet long, but no known shark grows that big. Only the Megalodon matched that size.

Another giant shark—much smaller than the Megalodon, but still huge by normal shark standards—is known as *Megamouth*. No one even suspected that this species of shark existed until 1976, when a research team working in Hawaii caught one by accident. It was 14.5 feet long and weighed 1,650 pounds. The team nicknamed it "Megamouth" because of its very large mouth, and that became its official scientific name. Several more have been caught since then, all male. Then in 1994, a female Megamouth shark washed ashore in Japan.

The Megamouth is so rare that in the past thirty years only thirty-eight have been seen or captured. When scientists studied the first one back in 1976, they realized it was unlike any other shark on earth (it was so large)—one of the most important dis-coveries in the study of fish in the twentieth century. They even

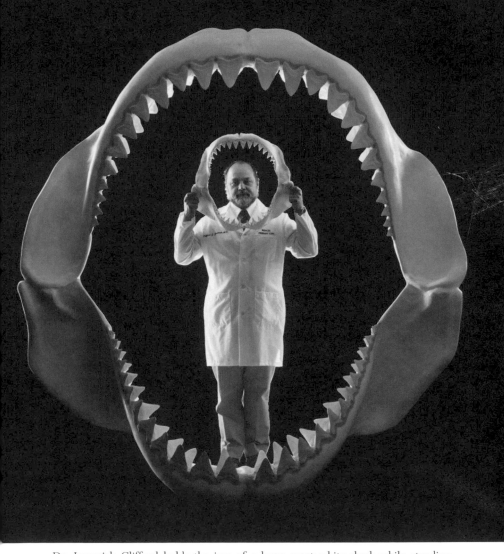

Dr. Jeremiah Clifford holds the jaw of a large great white shark while standing inside the reconstructed jaw of a Megalodon. (© LOUIE PSIHOYOS / CORBIS)

gave it its own species name: *Megachasma pelagios*, which means "great yawning mouth of the open water."

And in the nineteenth century, remains of a creature known as the *frilled shark* were discovered near Japan. The beast looked like a six- to eight-foot-long eel, with several gills that resemble frills, and the head of a shark. This creature was so rare (and strange looking—it looks like a fossil of an ancient creature) that most people believed it was extinct. Then, in 2007, local fishermen told staff at Japan's Awashima Marine Park in Shizuoka that they had found a strange-looking eel with extremely sharp teeth. Staff at the marine park managed to catch and film the shark, but it died a few hours later.

GIANT SNAKES

Giant beasts don't only live in the water or fly in the air. For over a hundred years, explorers and natives have encountered the *giant anaconda*, or *Sucuriju Gigante*, an enormous snake that lives in the Amazon rainforest, the swamps and rivers of the dense forests of tropical South America, and the southern swamps of Trinidad.

The name anaconda may come from the Sinhalese name for the snake, "henakanday," which means "whip snake," or the name used in the Tamil language, "anaik-konda," which means "elephant killer." The name Sucuriju Gigante comes from the native name for the creature, which means "giant water snake." Natives of the region also tell stories of a monster named *Sucuriju*, a giant snake that controls the rivers and swamps where it lives.

Most normal anacondas are around twenty feet long, and they can easily kill and eat a human being. The largest known anacondas were thirty feet long. But giant anacondas like Sucuriju Gigante are nearly twice that size.

One of the most famous giant anaconda sightings occurred in 1906, when an explorer named Perry Fawcett shot and wounded a snake that was sixty-two feet long—so big, in fact, that Fawcett couldn't carry it back out of the jungle. Another giant anaconda was spotted in 1925 by a priest named Father Victor Heinz on the Rio Negro in the Amazon. He said the beast was over eighty feet long, with a body as thick as an oil drum.

Photo evidence of the Sucuriju Gigante first appeared in 1948, when a newspaper in Pernambuco, Brazil, published a picture with a headline "Anaconda Weighing 5 Tons." The picture showed a giant anaconda over 100 feet long, with a half-swallowed bull in its mouth. Four months later, a newspaper in Rio de Janeiro published a photo of an anaconda that was 115 feet long. And in 1959, a helicopter pilot managed to take photos of a giant anaconda that had risen out of the water to attack him as he was flying over the Katanga province of the Belgian Congo. That snake was fifty feet long.

Unfortunately, no one has ever been able to capture one of these creatures, and until then, the largest officially recognized anaconda on record remains thirty-two to thirty-three feet long—tiny by comparison.

Four members of the Matses Indian tribe hold up an eighteen-foot-long anaconda. (© JEFFREY L. ROTMAN/CORBIS)

CHUPACABRAS AND
6. OTHER MYSTERIOUS
MONSTERS

Some of the scariest and most mysterious monsters in the world don't fit into any category. They aren't like Bigfoot or the Loch Ness Monster, and they aren't giant versions of regular animals. Many people believe that some of the strange creatures in this chapter might even be aliens from other planets! A few of these monsters didn't appear until this century, while others date back to mythological times. Some are dangerous and even deadly, and some are just plain weird.

THE CHUPACABRA

The name *Chupacabra* means "goat-sucker" in Spanish. As you may be able to guess, the creature known as Chupacabra is known for attacking livestock (mostly goats) and drinking the animals' blood.

Witnesses usually describe the beast as three to five feet tall, and they say it hops like a kangaroo. In some cases, it's been known to hop as far as twenty feet in a single jump. It looks like a lizard or a small dinosaur, with greenish-gray leathery skin (some say it has scales on its skin, while others have even reported seeing it covered in gray fur), and sharp spines along its back, like porcupine quills, which it uses to fly. It has two small arms and three fingers with claws on each hand.

EACH ANIMAL HAD TWO PUNCTURE HOLES IN ITS NECK, AND MOST OF ITS BLOOD WAS GONE.

The Chupacabra's oval-shaped head has a long jaw, making its face look a little like a dog or a panther, and it has a forked tongue. Its eyes are usually red, although sometimes they are a beady black, and some believe the creature can use them to hypnotize its prey. It has a small thin mouth with visible fangs, and when startled, the Chupacabra hisses and screeches at people, then jumps away, leaving behind a strong smell, like sulphur.

Some witnesses describe its ability to change colors, almost like a chameleon. In the dark, it changes its skin color to black or dark brown. In the daylight, if green trees and bushes are around, it may change its color to green, green-gray, light brown, or beige. Some believe that the creature is a half-human, half-animal vampire, while others say it's like a panther, except with red eyes and a snake's tongue. Some reports have even called it a cross between a dog and a reptile.

The modern mystery of the Chupacabra may have started in the 1970s when stories began to surface about the strange killings of different animals near the Puerto Rican town of Moco—where the monster was called *Vampire de Moco*—and in the township of Canóvanas. Birds, horses, and goats had all been found dead. Each animal had two puncture holes in its neck, and most of its blood was gone. This led many to believe there was a vampire in the area.

But it was a string of sightings starting in 1995 that made the Chupacabra phenomenon take off. The first was in Puerto Rico, where farmers reported finding some of their small farm animals killed and drained of blood, each with small punctures in its neck. In the town of San Germán, a group of townspeople claimed to have chased the creature away when they found it trying to catch some roosters. In Guánica, a man named Osvaldo Claudio Rosado said he had been attacked by a creature like a gorilla, while in Canóvanas a woman named Madeline Tolentino said she and her neighbors had seen a Chupacabra walking in the street in the middle of the afternoon! When they approached it, the creature ran away. The mayor gathered up a group to hunt for the monster. They went out each week for nearly a year, but never found it.

Over the next few years, Central and South American countries began to report similar animal deaths. Then Chupacabras began to appear in the United States, particularly in Texas, Maine, Hawaii, New York, Florida, and Oregon.

Although its popularity took off in the 1990s, the monster doesn't appear to be new. Native people in the rainforests of South America tell stories of a creature called the "mosquito man," which sucks the blood out of animals through a long nose, and legends of a similar creature in South American rainforests go back hundreds of years. No one knows why it suddenly began to make regular appearances in the early 1990s, but since 1995 the Chupacabra has been blamed for the deaths of over 2,000 farm animals, and has been reported as far away as Russia and Hawaii!

There are many theories about where the Chupacabras come from. Some believe they live in caves deep below the earth, while others think Chupacabras actually come from the future! Another story is that they were the pets of aliens who came to Earth a long time ago. Strangely enough, people have sometimes reported seeing UFOs near the locations of the animals that Chupacabras have fed on.

THE JERSEY DEVIL

Not many monsters are famous enough to have a National Hockey League hockey team named after them, but that's the case for the *Jersey Devil*, which is said to live in the Pine Barrens in southern New Jersey, where people have told stories about this creature for over 250 years.

The Jersey Devil, shown here, is said to inhabit the Pine Barrens in southern New Jersey. (© BETTMANN/CORBIS)

The most popular legend of the Jersey Devil concerns the thirteenth child of a woman named Mrs. Deborah Leeds, who lived in the Pine Barrens in the mid-eighteenth century. Mrs. Leeds was so upset at having another child that she asked the devil to take it. As soon as she made this offer, the baby grew wings, turned into a monster, and flew away through the chimney! There are many versions of this story. In some, the Jersey Devil was a normal human child who lived and grew up in the woods, only to later change and develop strange powers. In others, Mrs. Leeds was a witch who created the Jersey Devil using her magical powers.

The Lenni Lenape tribes called the Pine Barrens area "Popuessing," which means "place of the dragon." When Swedish explorers arrived, they called the area "Drake Kill" ("Drake" was another name for dragon), and by the mid-eighteenth century, settlers had begun to report sightings of the strange creature. They blamed it for killing their farm animals, and avoided the Pine Barrens as a desolate, threatening area.

The most famous series of encounters happened in 1909, when thousands of people claimed to see the Jersey Devil over the course of a single week. Sightings began on the sixteenth of January, when the creature was spotted flying over the city of Woodbury. Each day, people reported seeing it in the air, or finding strange footprints in the snow. On the nineteenth, a man named Nelson Evans saw the creature in front of his house. Nelson was scared, but managed to chase the monster off—it made a barking sound at him, and then flew away.

On the twenty-first of January, the Devil apparently attacked some trolley cars in the city of Haddon Heights. Later that day, it nearly attacked a group of people in West Collingswood, and even bit a poor dog in the city of Camden.

Reported sightings slowed down after that week, but they didn't stop. There have been hundreds of reports about the Jersey Devil since then, with dozens more being added each year. Witnesses describe the creature as being three to seven feet tall, with a head like a dog or a horse, and—according to some—the body of a human. It has a long neck, bat-like wings two feet long, short front legs, long hind legs with hooves on them, and a pointed tail. It walks on its hind legs, but seems to prefer flying. The Jersey Devil's eyes glow bright red, and it makes a high-pitched scream that sounds like a human's voice.

In most encounters, the creature screams and flies or runs away when it sees people. But it has occasionally chased people unlucky enough to find themselves walking through the Pine Barrens area at night.

THE BEAST OF GÉVAUDAN

One of France's most well-known monsters is the *Beast of Gévaudan*. This creature lived in the province of Gévaudan (in today's Lozère département), in the Margeride Mountains in south-central France from about 1764 to 1767. For many people, it's the French version of the Loch Ness Monster.

In the spring of 1764, a girl was working on a farm when she saw a large creature that looked like a giant wolf charge at her from the trees of the Forêt de Mercoire. Luckily, there were bulls in the field, and they were able to keep the beast from getting to her. Over the next three years, the beast attacked more people. Witnesses described it as a wolf the size of a cow, with a head that looked like a greyhound. The beast had large fangs, and could leap thirty feet.

In 1765, the King of France sent his best hunters to try to kill the beast. They searched for months, and finally killed a large gray wolf. The country celebrated, but a few months later the attacks began again. This time, hunters killed any wolf they saw, and panic spread across the countryside. Finally, in 1767, a hunter named Jean Chastel used silver bullets to slay a giant wolf-like creature, and the mysterious attacks stopped.

Unfortunately, no one knew where the body was buried, so there was no way to find out exactly what the beast was, until 1997, when a man named Franz Jullien, who worked at a museum in Paris, discovered an unusual stuffed animal in its collection. It was reported to have been a creature very similar to the infamous Beast of Gévaudan. When Franz studied the creature's fur, he found it was a striped hyena.

This seemed to solve the mystery of the beast (although no one knows how a large and dangerous creature like that ever arrived in France—striped hyenas live in Africa, the Middle East, Pakistan, and western India, and are extinct in Europe). But many other theories still remain: some believe the creature was a werewolf, while others say it was a type of wolf-dog, specially bred at that time for hunting.

Another popular theory is that the attackers were actually humans who used the story of wolf attacks to cover their own crimes. One reason for this comes from Jean Chastel's own story. Chastel claimed that before he shot the beast, he took out a Bible and prayed, and that the creature sat and waited for him to finish praying before they began their battle. This odd behavior caused many people to believe that Chastel had made the entire story up. (Some people even said that Chastel was actually behind the attacks, which stopped after he claimed to have killed the monster.) Other people believed that Chastel had trained or owned the creature, which would have simply attacked him right away if it was truly wild.

AN ANCIENT HYENA?

It is said that a creature similar to the Beast of Gévaudan attacked people in India and Ethiopia, but stories of this monster are at least two thousand years older than those of the beast. A cross between a dog and a wolf, and perhaps a hyena, the *Crocotta* (sometimes call the *Corocotta*, *Crocuta*, or *Yena*) had powerful teeth and hunted people and dogs by imitating the sounds of a person calling for help. It sometimes listened to farmers talking, and would call them into the woods to hunt them once it learned their names. Some said the creature could change its colors. Others said its eyes were like gems and that they could give you the power to see into the future if you held them under your tongue. But these are ancient legends, and there haven't been any recent sightings of the creature.

A CROSS BETWEEN A DOG AND A WOLF, AND PERHAPS A HYENA, THE CROCOTTA (SOMETIMES CALL THE *COROCOTTA, CROCUTA* OR *YENA*) HAD POWERFUL TEETH AND HUNTED PEOPLE AND DOGS BY IMITATING THE SOUNDS OF A PERSON CALLING FOR HELP.

A similar ancient creature called the *Leucrota*—a mix between the Crocotta and a lion—was also said to imitate human voices. The size of a donkey, the Leucrota was fast and vicious. It had the legs of a stag, and the tail, chest, and neck of a lion. Its head was shaped like a horse's, and its mouth could open as far back as its ears. It had no teeth, having a single long bone in their place, but it could crush anything in its powerful jaws. People said the Leucrota never closed its eyes, and could turn its head all the way around to see behind it. The local people treated it as a demon, and were very scared of encountering one.

They may be creatures of legends and myths, but many scientists now believe the Crocotta and Leucrota are actually descriptions of ancient hyenas. In fact, the scientific name of the spotted hyena (*Crocuta crocuta*) comes from the Crocotta. Hyenas also have powerful teeth and jaws, and they are know for making sounds that are eerily close to human voices (including their famous laugh).

GOATMEN

Sometimes the strangest creatures are actually a combination of rather common animals. One such creature is the *Goatman*.

The Goatman has mostly been seen in the area of Prince George's County in Maryland, although some hunters in 1972 reported seeing a Goatman creature in the East Texas town of Marshall. In California, there is the tale of the *Chevo Man* ("Chevo" is Spanish for goat). Other stories of Goatmen have also come in from Alabama, Oregon, Oklahoma, Kentucky, and even New Zealand.

Most of these stories describe encounters with a creature that's half-human, half-goat: the legs and feet of a goat, and the upper body of a human, with horns on its head. The creature is six to seven feet tall, weighs 300 pounds, and is covered in gray fur. Witnesses also say it makes very strange, high-pitched squealing noises.

In a recent sighting from 2000, a group of construction workers saw the Goatman in a suburb of Washington, D.C. The workers described it as twelve feet tall and hairy, looking almost like Bigfoot.

A Goatman-like creature known as the *Pope Lick Monster* haunts an area in Louisville, Kentucky. People believe this creature lives beneath the Pope Lick Trestle, which is a long, high, dangerous railway bridge over Pope Lick Creek in Louisville. Like the Goatman, the Pope Lick Monster is usually described as a beast with a human body and the head of a goat, although others say it has white fur and looks like a Yeti.

Several strange stories have built up around both of these creatures—in some they are the results of secret scientific experiments gone wrong, while in others they are supposed to be escaped patients from the local mental hospital. Still others claim the Goatman may be the father of the Chupacabra! While most of these stories are so far-fetched they're probably best kept for Halloween, the strange encounters continue to be reported.

THE WENDIGO

Many native tribes in North America describe a supernatural creature called the *Wendigo*.

Stories of it go back for centuries. Some say the Wendigo was once a powerful warrior who gave his life to save his tribe and whose spirit continues to wander the forests. Other stories agree that the monster was once human, but somehow changed and became the monster it is today. One story says you can only see it head-on because it's too thin to be seen from the side, while another claims that it's a giant with a heart of ice (sometimes the stories say its whole body is made of ice), and the only way to destroy it is to melt it.

Some people even believe the Wendigo is actually an evil spirit that can take over a person who is lost in the wild during the winter months. In fact, there were many "Wendigo trials" in Canada in the late 1700s, when people were accused of being Wendigos—much like the witch trials that took place in Europe.

In the seventeenth century, explorers and missionaries began to report encounters with this strange creature, which they described as a devil, or a werewolf with glowing eyes, large yellow fangs, and a long tongue. Sightings of the Wendigo have been rare since then, but many people believe the creature, or evil spirit, still haunts the forests of Canada in the wintertime.

AFTER NEWS OF THIS ATTACK GOT OUT, MANY MORE PEOPLE REPORTED SEEING AND BEING CHASED BY THE LIZARD MAN. THE POLICE EVEN HAD TO SET UP A LIZARD MAN HOTLINE TO HANDLE ALL THE PHONE CALLS.

THE LIZARD MAN

A strange creature known as the *Lizard Man of Scape Ore Swamp*, or *Lizard Man of Lee County*, lives in the swamps of Lee County, South Carolina.

In 1988, a young man named Christopher Davis was changing the tire on his truck when he heard a loud thump coming from the field behind him. When Christopher turned around, he saw a large creature with glowing red eyes running at him. Christopher got into his truck, but as he drove away, the creature jumped on the roof. Luckily, Christopher was able to shake the monster off the truck by speeding up and swerving sharply.

After news of this attack got out, many more people reported seeing and being chased by the Lizard Man. The police even had to set up a Lizard Man hotline to handle all the phone calls. After a few months, the sightings stopped as suddenly as they had started. Since then, there have only been a few reported sightings in that area.

Encounters with Lizard Men have also occurred elsewhere in the United States, usually when and where UFOs have been seen. In 1967, a police officer in Nebraska claimed to have been taken aboard a UFO, where he met a reptilian, human-shaped alien. Lizard men have also been spotted in the Superstition Mountains of Arizona, Dulce Base in New Mexico, and Mount Shasta in California.

According to reports, they are five and a half to nine feet tall. They have long arms with three long fingers and a thumb, and their feet have four toes with short, blunt claws. Lizard men are usually described as greenish-brown and covered with scales.

They have wide mouths, with no lips and sharp teeth. Their eyes are either large and black, with white pupils like vertical slits, or white with fiery red pupils in vertical slits.

Among the many, even stranger claims put forward about Lizard Men is that they are from another planet and have secretly guided the course of human civilization for thousands of years!

KAPPA

Ponds and rivers throughout Japan are home to the *Kappa*, a child-sized creature the looks like across between a human, a monkey, and a frog. In some cases, the Kappa have thick shells on their backs and scaly green, yellow, or blue skin. They have webbed hands and feet, and strange hollow dents filled with water on the top of their heads. It is believed that the Kappa get incredible strength from the water-filled dents on their heads and that they will become very weak if they spill the water.

Kappas are mischievous troublemakers and have been known to attack people. Because they are said to be afraid of fire, some villages hold fireworks festivals each year to scare them away. But even today, there are often signs in some Japanese towns and villages warning people about the dangerous Kappa.

LOVELAND FROG

In 1955, a group of human-like creatures with faces like frogs were seen under a bridge by a businessman in Loveland, Ohio. According to the man, the creatures were each around three feet tall, with wrinkles in their skin instead of hair, and wide mouths that looked like a frog's. One of them was holding a strange device that shot out sparks. They didn't attack the man, and vanished soon after he saw them.

The frogs were not seen again until 1972, when police in Loveland saw a four-foot-tall creature that looked like a human, but with the face of a frog and leathery green skin. Over the next few weeks, more and more sightings occurred—a police officer even chased after one and shot at it. He missed, and the creature disappeared in the forest.

The creature seemed to have gone away for good, until 1998, when a motel security guard in the Dominican Republic saw a five-foot-tall and three-foot-wide frog- and human-like being. It was near the motel, but it ran (or jumped) away when the guard approached it.

With creatures as strange as the Chupacabra, or as mysterious as Bigfoot and the Beast of Busco, it's often hard to tell the difference between a real encounter that someone is trying to describe, and a scary story that someone has made up. Usually, you can find a bit of both.

In some cases (like the giant squid), recent explorations have managed to prove that the monsters of old actually exist and still live today. In others (such as the Mothman), the mystery remains and may never be solved.

Whatever the truth may be, it's certainly fun to read about these unusual monsters and imagine what would happen if you encountered one. And remember, they could appear anywhere, so be sure to keep an eye out for them!

SOURCES

There are many great books and Web sites about cryptozoology and the different cryptids we have looked at in this book. If you're eager for more information about any of the cryptids we've examined, or if you want to find more of them, here are some great places to start.

BOOKS

Borges, Jorge Luis, with Margarita Guerrero and Norman Thomas di Giovanni. *The Book of Imaginary Beings*. New York: Avon Books, 1970.

Clark, Jerome, and Loren Coleman. *Cryptozoology A-Z*. New York: Simon & Schuster, 1999.

Coleman, Loren, and Patrick Huyghe. *Field Guide to Lake Monsters, Sea Serpents, and Other Mystery Denizens of the Deep*. New York: Tarcher, 2003.

Greer, John Michael. *Monsters: An Investigator's Guide to Magical Beings*. Woodbury, MN: Llewellyn Publications, 2001.

Hall, Mark A. *Thunderbirds: America's Living Legends of Giant Birds*. New York: Paraview Publishing, 2004.

Hines, Terence. *Pseudoscience and the Paranormal*. Amherst, NY: Prometheus Books, 2003.

WEB SITES

http://bestiary.ca: The Medieval Bestiary.

http://cusith.com: Cu Sith.

http://strangemaine.blogspot.com: Strange Maine.

www.americanmonsters.com: American Monsters.

www.bcscc.ca: The British Columbia Scientific Cryptozoology Club.

www.bigfootencounters.com: Bigfoot Encounters.

www.cbc.ca/news/background/fact or fiction: CBC News Indepth: Fact or Fiction?

www.cryptozoology.com: Cryptozoology

www.forteanzoology.com: The Centre for Fortean Zoology.

www.lclt.org: Lake Champlain Land Trust.

www.livescience.com: LiveScience.

www.lorencoleman.com: The Cryptozoologist.

www.louisvilleghs.com: The Louisville Ghost Hunters Society.

www.meta-religion.com: MetaReligion.

www.mokelembembe.com: Mokele Mbembe: The Living Dinosaur!

www.mysteriousworld.com: Mysterious World.

www.nessie.co.uk: The Legend of Nessie.

www.newanimal.org: The Cryptid Zoo.

www.occultopedia.com: The Occult and Unexplained Encyclopedia.

www.rfthomas.clara.net/bigfoot.html: Bigfoot: Fact or Fantasy?

www.storsjoodjuret.com

www.strangemag.com: Strange Magazine.

www.unmuseum.org: The Museum of Unnatural Mystery.

www.wyrdology.com: Wyrdology-Interesting Weird Stuff.

INDEX